REFLECTIONS
FROM A BROKEN
MIRROR

ANDREW BARBER

© Andrew Barber 2010

This edition first published in 2010 by
Forward Press Ltd
Remus House
Coltsfoot Drive
Woodston
Peterborough
PE2 9JX

Tel 01733 890099
Fax 01733 313524
www.forwardpress.co.uk

ISBN 978-1-84418-546-7

To Slayer,
Jodie and Kai

Hope you
enjoy this!
should be
something
for everyone,
kids
included!
Andy x

This book is dedicated to everyone who inspired
these poems, especially Shanta, Kashna and Esina.

The embrace of poetry like that of bodies,
As long as it lasts,
Shuts out any glimpse of the misery of the world.
André Breton

Most wretched men
Are cradled into poetry by wrong;
They learn in suffering what they teach in song.
Percy Bysshe Shelley

Andrew Barber beat thousands of other poets to become the inaugural Poetry Rivals Slam Champion in April 2010. He also won a Highly Commended award in the Margaret Reid Prize for Traditional Poetry and is poet-in-residence for Walford Web, an EastEnders website, where he writes regular poems about the show. This collection represents highlights from a twenty year writing career.

Acknowledgements

Thanks to Morgan, Lynsey and all at Forward Press.

Thanks to Katy Mascall for arranging transport to Peterborough for the *Poetry Rivals* final (thanks also to all the judges who chose my poem as the winner).

Thanks to Esina Barber for finding the *Poetry Rivals* competition online.

Thanks to Roger Waters, Bob Dylan, John Lennon, John Donne, Lewis Carroll, Douglas Adams and everyone else who made me want to write.

Thanks to my parents Alan and Shirley for teaching me to love the sung or written word.

Thanks to my photographers, Leela Panikar (front cover) and David Pratt (back cover).

And special thanks to Shanta for making me believe that everything was possible.

Foreword

Hello Reader,

Funny thing, life. Three months ago, I had no idea I'd be writing this, the foreword to my book. I didn't even know I'd have a book. Last year, my twelve-year-old daughter Esina found the *Poetry Rivals* competition online and suggested I enter it. Why not? It was free. I'd been writing for years but had done nothing with it. So I entered. When I got invited to the final, I saw it as an opportunity to hear some good poetry, maybe chat to some good poets, nothing more. So when I won, I was stunned. This book was my prize.

From 'The Money God' in May 1990 to 'The Cockerel' in August 2010, this collection reflects two decades of my life. There are poems of love and regret, hope and cynicism, humour and surrealism. May your journey through them be interesting.

I've also set several of these poems to music and recorded them as songs. Anyone who wants a more multimedia experience can find it at:

www.ReverbNation.com/ReflectionsFromABrokenMirror.

Andrew Barber

Contents

Lap Top Ovation

I sat you on my lap
And ran my fingers over your curves,
Your caramel colouring.

My left hand moved upwards
My thumb stroking the back of your neck
My fingers tracing complicated shapes on the front.

You moved slightly
And I heard a half-formed sound,
The music of the incomplete.

Fixed was my left hand,
Rhythmic was my right
As it pulsed over your hole
And the noise that started within you
Was the noise you were designed to make.
When we are joined together,
And even our voices co-mingle,
The world shrinks to the size of we two.

You know how to express my deepest fears,
My greatest joys and triumphs.
This would be the perfect relationship,
If you weren't a guitar.

Velvet with a Hint of Claw

I have a cat
Or should I say
My cat has me.
Sorry, John.

A wise man once said
That a dog has an owner,
A cat has staff.

How right he was.
How haughty is the cat,
How proud her disdain
And yet how great her need for us
To un-tin the mashed carcasses of sundry small creatures
For without us, she would die.

If she were a hunter, she would live
But she is a housecat,
Her hunting skills only tested against flies,
Moths,
A toy shaped optimistically like a zebra
And stationary, unattended meat on the kitchen counter.

What a piece of work is cat,
So nostalgic for her evolutionary history,
Like a Swede who acts like an emperor
Because his ancestors once ruled Europe.

What a contradiction is cat,
Soft and furry with a pleasing sound
Yet ruthlessly murderous when she remembers how,
Velvet with a hint of claw.

The Strophic Form for Dummies

Here's some words that fit the form
Those strophic, catastrophic rules:
Where's the chorus and the bridge?
Simplistic histories
Of nursery rhymes and mysteries
Evoke an age of plagues and roses,
Morris men with bloodshot noses,
A pensioner's dementia,
And ninety-nine green bottles in the fridge.

Downer Miner

When you show me the day
I remember the night.
I see the shadow
When you see the light.
I bring up the last
When you tell me the first.
You show me the best
And I point out the worst.

I'm a downer miner
And every silver lining has a cloud.

You give me the ointment,
I give you the fly.
You love to live,
I'm just waiting to die.
You tell me the value,
I think of the cost.
You're proud of the found,
I'm bemoaning the lost.

I'm a downer miner.
I know the good times pass.
I'm a downer miner
And I've never seen a half-full glass.

When your pedal's to the metal,
I'm the foot on the brakes.
I notice grocer's apostrophes
And grammatical mistakes.
I go and read a book
When you party on, dude.
I'm the beta blocker for your heart,
The Hoover for your mood.

I'm a downer miner.
I let the good times pass.
I'm a downer miner
And I've never seen a half-full glass.

If I haven't got a problem,
I can find one somewhere.
If I haven't got it on the ground,
I'll pluck it from the air.
If I can't find one at all,
That's not a problem, señor.
I'll grow it in a Petri dish
And throw it on the floor.

I'm a downer miner.
I make the good times pass.
I'm a downer miner
And I've never seen a half-full glass.
I'm a downer miner
And every silver lining has a cloud.

Knowing Jack

(Jack Branning is the playboy ex-policeman in EastEnders)

Jack had loved his brother's wife,
The black girl
And the blonde one
And her sister (who got pregnant)
And their cousin, who, if anything,
Was even blonder still.
I've seen him in the club
And in the Square and in a coma
But I've never really met him:
I think I never will.

And yet I know him so well.

I know his family, his history,
Assorted tales of woe,
A man of mystery,
James Bond with an E20 postcode.

I know Jack better
Than some of my closest friends
Because they don't come into my home
Four nights a week,
Telling me their stories,
Giving me a window to their lives
And emphasising significant moments with a drum roll.

Or do they?
I was forgetting about Facebook.
I've come to think of Facebook
Not as a telephone but a television,
Not a communications tool
But an entertainment medium,

Each 'friend' a channel,
Each post a programme,
An episode of the soap opera of their lives.

Yes, I have friends who are like Newsnight,
Like Horizon or Arena,
Discussing high-falutin' ideas
From a position of authority.
But I also have friends who are like EastEnders,
Like Shameless or Skins or Jeremy Vile,
Car crash TV reduced to bile,
Misspelt polemic
And relationship status updates
On an hourly basis
Long into the night.

Do I really know them?
Or is this like applying graphology to a signature,
Doomed to fail
Because the public face of someone
Only shows what they want to be seen?

Do I know Jack? Or do I 'know Jack'?

Sing a Song of Facebook

Hello stranger.
I know several people that you do too.
Can I be friends with you?

Hello stranger.
We've never met before
But you know Will and Sián
And a bunch of folk I swore
I'd keep in touch with.
Can I keep in touch with you?

I promise I won't bother you
With daft requests for guns.
I don't play those stupid games.
I'm just looking for someone
That I can talk to.

I hope that won't sound clingy.
I'm not the stalking kind
But I like a conversation
With people that I find
Common ground with,
And Facebook's good at that.
So please accept my friend request
And join me for a chat.

Sing a song of Facebook
A pocket full of rye
An inbox full of messages
As status updates fly
Before they vanish
To the hell of 'older posts'
And no one ever sees again
What anybody wrote.

I sit here with my laptop
And I feel my spirits sag.
I'm waiting like a Marxist
For the magical red flag
To be hoisted.
Have I got a friend request?
Has anybody commented
On what I've written yet?

No, there's nothing.
I just had a YouTube tab
And that's also got a red bit
That looks just like a flag.
I would close it
But it would take too long to load
When I want to see again
Whatever video I chose.
What was the video?
Some link I got: who knows?

I joined another group today.
I want a downward thumb.
There are millions of members.
Will the management succumb
To what the users want?
Isn't that the point?
To listen to the people,
Make them feel they have a choice?

But never mind that!
Someone's commented on what
I've had to say. I'd better see
If they like it or not.
Wait for the modem...
God, the Internet is hell.
Loading, loading...

Oh, they said 'lol'.

Sing a song of Facebook
A pocket full of hope.
But the great communicator
Says 'lmfao'.
Here's an emoticon.
Oh, did you really want a chat?
I'm just a stranger
And you're alone in your flat.

Eyes

Give me the eyes of a child
And I'll tell you what's really there.

Give me eyes that can see
With honesty and imagination:
My own eyes are too old.

All my life I've been making
Filters for my eyes,
Censoring the things
That contradict what I know,
What I think I know,
What I think I am.

I used to think that seeing these things
Would make me mad:
Now I realise that I was already mad.

But how am I to learn
If I can't see what I don't expect?

Give me the eyes of a child
And I will see with a sense of wonder
And I will see the point.

Secret Diary of a Hyperpower, Aged 234 ¾

I am America.

I am talking to myself
Because there is nowhere else here.
I am the only country on Earth.

The bits that aren't America
Are a theme park for America's benefit:
World World.

I host the World Series
And only America plays
Because as the song says
We are the world.
We could feed the world
But we don't.

I am America,
E pluribus unum,
Many unite into one.
But this is not quite true.

I am divided
By wealth, blood and race,
Apartheid on many levels,
Only united geographically.

I am troubled.
Sometimes I do things
I know I shouldn't do
And then wonder why I did them.

I like toys,
Loud, explosive toys
And I play with them
Wherever I like.

I am America.
Get used to it.

The Cockerel

Cock-a-doodle-don't
Wake me today.
Last night's chianti is still in my veins
And the stars were fading when I
Started to sleep.

Don't tell me the sun
Has cocked its head over the horizon.
My head is still beneath the sheets.

Your day has begun:
Tell someone who cares.
My day starts when my feet hit the floor,
Not when the sun hits the sky.

Think you rule the roost, do you?
Strut for the hens if you must:
It means nothing to me.
Your caterwauling is as
A wheel-spin in a pub car park,
A showy display of masculinity
That don't impress me much.

Watch your back, cockerel boy.
You have the morning
But I have the axe.

Arnie's Soliloquy

To bleed, or not to bleed; that is the question.
Whether the foe is the foe that dies to spatter
The wings and talons with uncaged abortion
Or to break down in a silicon huddle
In a dry component's ending. Goodbye creep,
Or four, and for a creep to slay I'd spend
My parting and my last few Aryan locks,
My precious hair-do. I'm an aberration
Proud to be unleash'd. No crying, creep,
Don't weep, except to scream.

Hamlet was described as
'The first action hero'
When I was described as the last
And yet I spent a term-in-a-tortured kindergarten
And got myself pregnant.
Truly those were the end of days.

For who would bear the whips of fate
That taunt this burly Austrian?
A million ducats every word
And every word a syllable.
The steroids that I'm sated with
Have robbed me of testosterone.
My biceps are like Heracles,
'Tis shame about the genitals.

But the end of one day
Is the beginning of the next.
Now I am old and fat
And I'm sagging like my pecs
There's always politics.
The Democrats like stars.

Republicans like gunmen.
And everyone likes cars:
I've got a Humvee
So everybody knows
That Arnie's coming through,
When I drive them off the road.

So now I am Governor
And everything's on track
And if I can't reach the White House
Don't worry, I'll be back
To California
Sun-kissed land of grape and vine.
But I warn you:
Don't try having a good time...

The Rocket Science Theory of Relationships

Once, when I was a young man,
I read a book on rocket science,
A somewhat dry tome on payload and thrust ratios,
Propulsion limited by the weight of the fuel,
Its combustion efficiency
And the speed with which it leaves the Earth.

Now I am older,
It puts me in mind of love.

Sometimes, like a rocket,
We move too slow,
And our love has not the strength
To escape the 'surly bonds of earth',
Bringing us crashing down,
To the sea, if we're lucky,
The ground if we're not,
Terminal velocity leaving us as a pile
Of broken components on the desert floor.

Sometimes we move too fast,
And leave the Earth's gravitational field so completely,
Our momentum keeps us going,
Leaving behind the ground
And all that keeps us grounded
As we carry on through space,
Still the victim of gravity
But not that of the Earth,
Like a comet, an asteroid,
Looking beautiful from a distance
But, in context, lost.

And sometimes we get it right
Locked in geostationary orbit around another,
Locked in step like a North Korean soldier,
Or the two bright bodies of a binary star,
A satellite orbiting
At the rotational speed of the Earth
So our relationship,
Our relativity,
Is right and doesn't need to change.

But usually,
We never know if we are going too fast
Or too slow
Until it is too late to change our speed.

Given the choice,
I would go too slow,
Taking my chances with the two to one odds
Of missing water when I fell,
Rather than the hundred percent chance
Of drifting through lonely and airless space
Until I hit something
That would destroy me.

But what do I know?
The closest I get to leaving the Earth
Is climbing the flight of stairs to my flat
Where I live alone,
Practising with paper aeroplanes,
And dreaming of the day
When I dare to fly again.

I Believe in Love

You brush your hair from your face
And the sun comes out and warms us both
I hesitate because I've been this way before
I know the warning signs
I know the score

You close your eyes to paint the lids
And the sun goes back behind the clouds
It might be time to re-evaluate some doubts
It's not a time to be alone

With your witchy ways
You've found a way to help me to forget
Those lonely Saturdays
Or maybe they just haven't happened yet
I didn't plan it
These things happen off the cuff
But now I believe in love

You taught me what I'm looking for
And I can't hide it anymore
I need your love
I need your presence in my life
Your effervescence and your light
To drive the shadows back
And keep the ghosts away
Bleed me some colour from the grey

I've been burnt too many times
To miss the subtext of the lie
It's a survival skill
I taught myself not to trust
The candied words I'd heard from love
I told myself I never will

I was an apostate for love
An unbeliever with a grudge
You made a convert out of me
You're my Damascus Boulevard
The face of Elvis in the yard
Where I spilt my tea

And with your witchy ways
You've found a way to help me to forget
Those lonely Saturdays
Or maybe they just haven't happened yet
I didn't plan it
These things happen off the cuff
But now I believe in love

For Kashna

Where have you gone, my brown-eyed girl?
It seems like only hours have passed
Since I threw you in the air
And caught you again,
Your giggles spurring both of us to play
For longer than we should
In the sunshine of your infancy.

Where have you gone, my brown-eyed girl?
Just a few minutes ago,
I skated with you to school,
Disassembling your scooter
And riding back with it on mine,
Before returning
To re-assemble it for the journey home
When you first went out to school.

Where have you gone, my brown-eyed girl?
Seconds ago at most,
We were talking about music,
Sharing favourite tracks,
You singing along,
Me learning those you really like
So I could play them for you,
In the ever-changing landscape of your adolescence.

Where have you gone, my brown-eyed girl?
You have grown,
No longer my girl
But your woman,
Independent of thought and word and deed,
Ready to face the world and its challenges.

I could not be more proud.

Love Is...

Love is the cheese in sex's mousetrap.
Love is the blindfold that lets you see with your memories.
Love is the mirror that shows what should be,
Not what is.
Love is the last gasp of a dying cynicism.
Love is the god that strides the heart
Like an earthquake in clown shoes.
Love is the plant that grows in the shit of a crow
And must be watered with blood.
Love is hope,
Disguised in the camouflaged clothes of a soldier.
Love is the sun,
Reflected in the tears of a child.
Love is the grail, the goal,
The target, the soul.
Love is the cash cow,
Dry-humped to the point of red-raw exhaustion
By Interflora, Hollywood and Hallmark.
Love is the salesman for forgiveness.
Love just *is*.

Four-way Acrostic? Maybe I Love You!
(Inspired by a double acrostic written by Lewis Carroll)

As smooth as a Queen's Counsel with a horsehair head;
No fossil knows the fruit of an Oriental worm.
Down the Road of history the Asian merchants tread;
Down the road to Africa where jackals swarm.
Other creatures too: shy, enabled, cruel,
Never stopping laughing long enough to eat.
The maniac cessation of the entry rule
Files credit card as database when meanings meet.
Open up all areas! It sounds like excess,
Reaching for the top of the map, for the pole.
Get a new direction, or the magnets do the rest.
Everything is grim up there, like Oliver, I'm told.
Total up your fingers, as often as you ken:
Every time there's tension in the test.
So, X is for Roman? The German must be Zen.
Incontinence? It's one of the best.
Name as short as any but it's home to the most.
As I am a gweilo, can I be your ghost?

This 18 line poem contains clues to 6 words. Each word has 3 lines of hints, e.g., lines 1 - 3 relate to word 1. These 3 lines also contain the answer, as in a Wordsearch. E.g., the word 'henna' might be hidden in the phrase 'when nature calls'.

Taking the first and last letters of these 6 words will give 2 more words. There are also two hidden messages.

The solution is on the next page.

Solution

Lines	Answer	Found in:
1 - 3	Silk	fos*sil k*nows
4 - 6	Hyena	s*hy ena*bled
7 - 9	Access	mani*ac cess*ation
10 - 12	North	directio*n or the*
13 - 15	Ten	of*ten* and *ten*sion
16 - 18	Asia	*as I am*

Reformatting the answers gives the following:

```
S   I   L   K
H Y E N A
A C C E S S
N O R T H
T   E   N
A   S   I   A
```

Shanta and Kashna are the names of my wife and eldest daughter.

But don't I have two daughters? Yes, which is why the first letter of each line of the poem spells out:

'And don't forget Esina', who is my youngest daughter.

There are three acrostics described above, But the title calls this poem a four-way acrostic. Is it wrong?

No, because 'Four-way Acrostic? Maybe I Love You!' spells out 'family', which is what the whole exercise is about.

Love is a Coelacanth

Like a bloodhound I wooed,
Finding a scent, sniffling and slobbering.
Like a pig with the whiff of truffles decorating his snout,
Inciting and indicting his purpose.

I did not find love.

Like a penguin I wooed,
With suits like Cary Grant,
Cute like Carrie Fisher,
Slick like Peter Mandelson
Being pulled from within a duck.

I did not find love.

Like a caveman I wooed,
A cowboy,
A chest-beating volcano of molten testosterone,
Tarzan, Rambo and King Kong combined.

I still did not find love.

I thought I found love once
But every truck looks like a Ferrari
When you stand by the side of the road too long.

I stopped looking for love
And then love found me.

An instant flash of recognition,
A consensus ad idem,
And the Earth tilted,
Not with calamity and earthquake
But with the sure and certain knowledge that
all was now right with the world.

If you still haven't found what you're looking for,
Stop looking.
Seek and ye shall not find,
If what ye seek is love.
The act of observing changes the observed.
The act of seeking changes the seeker,
Making him less likely to keep what he seeks
If he finds it.

Relax.

Wait.

Think of something else.

Love is not a whale that can be harpooned.
It is not even a trout that can be caught by tickling.

Love is a salmon,
Swimming against the current,
Proud and contrary.

Love is a coelacanth,
Cropping up unexpectedly from the depths of the ocean,
The depths of time.

Love is the scarlet flower
That blossoms four miles deep
Where there is no light to see it.

Love is not a housepet that comes when it is called.
It is a gift to those who are ready for it.

Written in Response to a Corporate Email Request, in Verse, to Give Blood

'Twas on a winter even-night
That first I read the email rhyme,
Amidst the dull irrelevance
Of memos and position sheets,
It seemed to shine, a beacon glow,
Not out of place but out of time.
Reminder of an olden day
When language had an oath to keep.

A breath of fragrant air it was,
So different from the usual crap
Polluting my computer with its ramblings:
I've had enough!
The answer's yes, my blood is yours
I've gallons here, just turn the tap,
I doubt that I will miss it,
I've donated all the other stuff.

My faith, my hope, my sanity
Have long been bartered for a wage.
A mortgaged millstone drags me down
To drown beneath the acid flood.
I've cut my hair and donned a suit
And bought a timeshare in a cage.
It seems a little selfish if
I still insist I keep my blood.

So take it all, my organs too
My ulcers and my haemorrhoids,
My lungs may still be useful
If not poisoned by the London air.

The spleen, the liver, eyes and ears
May still be gainfully employed.
I'll save my soul for Judgement Day;
Whatever's left is yours to share.

Nathan and Roxie Win the Lottery

The miracle occurred
And God was nowhere to be seen:
Only biology was needed,
And probability,
As the one in thirty million chance
Paid off.

Maybe the lottery isn't so hard after all.

And clinging parasitically to the uterine wall,
A redividing collection of cells
Begin their journey towards life.

First one cell,
Then a couplet,
Then a quartet,
And soon
A heart, eyes, lungs and fingers,
Evolution in real time,
All the majesty of nature
Coalescing into nine months of cellular programming.

How can something so commonplace
Be so miraculous?

Because the gift of life
Is the greatest gift of all
And you get it for free.

The Lost Parade

Do you see us
From the corner of your eye,
When you look through us?
Do you know we're there,
Beside you but not of you,
Living on a tangent,
Living on a scrapheap,
Hidden between the cracks and the shadows?

Seek and you will find.
We are there,
Fireworks awaiting the caress of a spark,
Dressing in the costumes of a pantomime
Or a history book,
So that you may see us
As we see ourselves,
Not wrong but different,
Not mad but not conforming
Except to the camaraderie
Of the Lost Parade.

Brief Encounter

I stood at the lights
And in the middle distance,
I saw a face I recognised,
A face I'd seen on screen.

The April sun flashed
In a puddle left by the April rain,
And the light flooded my retina,
Forced me to consider
Who the face could be?

Dark hair, mutton chops,
And a handlebar moustache...
Lemmy?
The nameless bad guy
From a thousand bad Westerns?
And then it struck me:
This was a friend of mine from Facebook,
One I'd never met,
Randomly chosen for the commonality of our mutual friends
And the presumption of our shared interests.

This was a first for me.

I had thought of Facebook
And the physical world
As distant as Heaven and Earth,
Each reflecting the other,
But one real and one just an idea.

And now,
Like Roger Rabbit gaining an extra dimension,
A character had crossed between worlds
And become real,

Assumed human form and mannerisms,
Like an actor,
Shorn of his make-up and costume,
Free from the shackles of script,
A person where once was a cipher,
A dramatised construct.

So we met, and shook hands,
By the side of the road,
And we spoke,
Learned beard to learned sideburns.

And what did we speak of?
We spoke of Facebook,
Commenting on each other's posts
Like we were still online,
Talking of those who think
A photo of a motorbike
Represents them better than their own face.

Was this real life?
Or was this Facebook by other means,
A different platform
And a more interactive interface?

I did not have the chance to find out.
It was my daughter's birthday
And I had to rush home for cake.

Interesting Times

History rides a Ferris wheel, diplomacy a tank.
The has-been and the never-will take arms across a riverbank.
The TV shows the pictures and the PC gets the mail.
The faceless sell the useless to the vacuous for hours.

The DVD's been re-released, the CD's in the tray.
The toaster in the kitchen has been checked for Y2K.
Chocolate eggs cost fifteen pence, real ones twenty-five.
The madness of the marketplace demands what is supplied.

Time and space are convalescing,
Alchemy turns black to gold.
Sumericans from Babylondon
Use the news to break the old.
Double plus disintegration
Coming to you live.
We live in interesting times.

I caught the whiff of sulphur on a zephyr from Iraq.
The brimstone fell like lepers, in the desert, in the dark.
The H_2O exploded into H_2SO_4.
The Winnebago's loaded with provisions for the war.

The clock is ticking midnight as the insights get surreal.
The thirteenth angry penguin has upset the seventh seal.
The Horsemen have reformed and are rehearsing for the tour,
Accessing all areas with 'All the Hits... And More'.

John had Revelations, Jude had sleepless nights,
George had his relations selling merchandising rights.
Tony played Salome while Langley drew Baghdad
And underneath the netting there were boxes under flags.

Time and space are decompressing,
Industry turns green to black.

Diplomacy turns tail and scarpers.
No one goes to get it back.
Double plus disinformation
Infiltrates your mind.
We live in interesting times.

Time and space will die intestate,
History turns black to white.
Peace exists in isolation
Haunted by the will to fight.
Double plus dictators spin updated alibis.
We live in interesting times.

Razor Blades and Sunlight

Sat on the roof watching clouds go by
In the rain
And my spaniel stiffened,
Sniffed at the air like a roller blind,
Roller skates,
Razor blades and sunlight
Fall through the gap from the cumulus
To my brain:
I cocked my ears and listened,
Looked to the street by the building site
In the rain
And the rainbow glistened.

Looking down
I thought I was the only one.
Looking back
I was wrong.

Walked down the street with my jacket on
I was cold
And the rainbow shivered:
Just lost a bet with the leprechaun
For the gold
But he doesn't give a
Damn he's got all that he really wants
Why have more?
Doesn't seem to matter.
Just needs the rain and a beam of light
And a cloud
Just to be dramatic.

Looking up
I thought I was the only one.
Looking back
I was wrong.

The Photograph Fell

The photograph fell, and descending,
The bullets of light from the window
Cast lazy prismatics away to the wall.

It fell to the floor, and its bevelled edge cracked
And sent shards of itself to fall glittering,
Suddenly dancing perversely,
Suddenly spearing the pile of the Axminster shag.

A particle larger than most landed blunted edge downwards,
The razor side topmost to skewer
The sepia inmates of Yesterdayland.

The subjects within were asundered, dismembered,
The happy occasion of yesteryear's join
Separated at last by the ghost of the glass.

The image of bridal confetti no longer a record,
No longer a statement of love everlasting,
No longer a matter of pride,
Just a pile to be hoovered away.

The cat entered gaily,
And gamely attempted to conquer the carpet:
He bled all the way.

Love is ephemeral,
Its life can be measured in minutes,
Its grave just torn paper and glass,
The remains of the frame.
Its memory, however,
Will live on forever,
Deterring the wise
And ensnaring the rest.

Some things are best left unsaid.

Identity Crisis (The Credit Crunch Song)

Several socio-economic acronyms are used in this song. A yuppie is a 'young urban professional', a dinkie stands for 'double income, no kids', a sitcom is 'single income, two kids, oppressive mortgage' and a ninja stands for 'no income, no job or assets'. No references to Japanese assassins should be inferred.

I'm a banker
You see my type throughout the land
With our skinny mochaccinos
In our manicured hands.

I'm a banker
And I like to make my sport
Out of buying Lamborghinis
And selling short.

I'm a banker
And it's been sunshine all my life
From my twenty roomed apartment
To my second trophy wife.

I'm a banker
But now there's storm clouds in the sky.
The market has collapsed
And we can only wonder why.

We had the Eighties
When 'greed was good'.
We all believed it.
I wonder if we should.
I walked on Wall Street
Where the sun had shone.
I saw the rainbow
But the gold had gone.

I've been a yuppie, I've been a dinkie,
I've been a sitcom. I've had a dot-com.
I've been a ninja since everything went wrong.
And when the market crashed, I was unprepared:
I had my pension in HBOS shares.
I'm too poor for my wife
And now she's gone,
Gone.

I was a banker,
I was a master of the Earth.
I sold the worthless to the witless
When I knew what it was worth.

I was a banker
And now I wear a cardboard hat.
Here's your burger:
Do you want fries with that?

We had the Eighties
When 'greed was good'.
We still believe it.
I wonder if we should.
I walked on Wall Street
Where the sun had shone.
I saw the rainbow
But the gold had gone.

Away in a Manger

Away in a manger,
Mary told Joe
Her baby had come from above,
Not below.

Joseph went mental
And called her a slag.
Now he's got an ASBO
And his ankle is tagged.

Away in a manger,
Their fractious dispute
Attracted the presence
Of carers in suits.

They said that the manger
Was 'unfit for use';
Unhealthy, unsafe
And unsanitary too.

The cattle are mooing
In polls for The Sun.
A herd of complainers
Don't know what they've done.

Away in a manger,
They've taken away
The little lord Jesus
They called 'Baby J'.

His parents could buy him
No crib for a bed.
So now he's been fostered
By Herod instead.

Glastonberry Fool

A, B, C, D, E,
Once I went to Glastonbury.
F, G, H, I, J,
Then I had to go away.
K, L, M, N, O,
Tell me why you had to go?
P, Q, R, S, T,
Because I took some LSD.
U, V, W,
Tell me how it troubled you?
Woof, wibble, X, Y, Z,
I hear voices in my head.

Stitching Starlight to a Dream

I was lying in my garret, tying carrots to my stick,
Resenting misspent sentiment and the life it likes to pick,
When I thought I heard the flutter of a phoenix from the flames
As the ashes of a memory felt the stain of life again.

The duvet danced with fire as the phantom sang anew,
As an embryonic counterpoint to a melody I knew.
Demonic yet benevolent, oh deity repressed,
Merely humour me my dreamings and I'm blinded to the rest.

Oh Hope be thee my shepherd, lead me
through thy pastures green
On the promise of a maybe stitching starlight to a dream.
Come and ring me through my bloodied nose and lead me ever on.
He who pied the piper culled the tune; by the
time I'd started dancing it had gone.

And so the music stopped, and I was left without a seat.
I was exiled to the window, where I gazed down to the street,
To see the features of an angel hold aloft a septic smile
While a leprous finger summoned me to reminisce a while.

Reliving cherished memories, resurrecting ancient dreams,
Rewriting history line by line as I'd hoped it might have been.
Reciting tired mantras, reuniting ying and yang,
I'll submit my soul to servitude, and the song the siren sang.

Oh Hope be thee my shepherd, lead me
through thy pastures green
On the promise of a maybe stitching starlight to a dream.
Come and ring me through my bloodied nose and lead me ever on.
He who pied the piper culled the tune; by the
time I'd started dancing it had gone.

Venus in a Thunderbird, a symphony in blonde,
A choir singing sonnets to a paradise beyond.
The music bade me eagerly to take the floor again
When Messrs. Doubt and Paranoia came to visit and remain.

I couldn't help but notice that I've been this way before;
Even déjà vu's familiar down the road my footsteps wore,
But as the glimmer of a maybe reasserts itself as flame,
Casting caution to the furnace, I walk down the road again.

Oh Hope be thee my shepherd, lead me
through thy pastures green
On the promise of a maybe stitching starlight to a dream.
Now I think I hear the music, but the audience is weak.
Now the ears are fully functional, the voice
has lost the confidence to speak.

Metamorpheus

I'll see you in another lifetime
We might be cats or we might be giants
Throw me down another lifeline
I've got to make a noose
Hanging round in this sea of troubles
Knowing up from the stream of bubbles
Rosetta Stone met Barney Rubble
Playing fast and loose

And when the winter wind is blowing in
I think of you this way
The breeze beneath the door is ever more
Intrusive every day
The pile of books that I will never read
Topples to the floor
Broken promises in cemeteries
I've heard them all before

Underground but over water
A pair of Henry's for a farmer's daughter
She started running but I think I caught her
Fractionally late
Nine tenths of the law's perception
Break the mirror for a new reflection
Extra time for introspection
Write it off to fate

And when the winter wind is blowing in
I think of you this way
The breeze beneath the door is ever more
Intrusive every day
The pile of books that I will never read
Topples to the floor
Broken promises in cemeteries
I've heard them all before

I'll see you in La Nova Vita
We might be cats or some other creature
Hold on tight 'cause I'm gonna meet you
Where you're gonna be
Romeo and Juliet
I'll be the Montague to your Capulet
I've got a lute but I can't play it yet
My Persephone

And when the winter wind is blowing in
I think of you this way
The breeze beneath the door is never more
Intrusive than today
The pile of books that I will never read
Topples to the floor
Broken promises in cemeteries
I've heard them all before

Flowertimes

It's flowertime
For the cemetery wolf
The lupines rose to set the clocks
To three quarter time
The Straussmen start the waltz
The Viennese whirl round
The mirrored room
Cobwebs in the corner of the cellar
Catch the colour of the moon

Amadeus lifts his fingers from the keys
Listens to the howling on the wind
That blows its rhythm through the trees
A pipistrelle swoops dancing
Through the night
Back-lit by the lightning forking overhead
And lightening the sky

Amadeus gets ideas from time to time
And when the lightning comes
The inspiration falls on him like rain
And then the morning comes again

The cemetery wolf
Preying on the memories in the graves
Catches one and takes it to the cave
To make a sacrifice
It comes down with the rain
Like a lightning strike
Directly to the brain
Amadeus wakes
It starts again

It's flowertime
For the cemetery wolf
Who woos the muse with lupines
And then wounds her horse
Amadeus goes to bed
Tries to take a nap
But he knows
It comes back

Amadeus gets ideas from time to time
And when the lightning comes
The inspiration falls on him like rain
And then the morning comes again

Food Chain Reactions

We the undecided use a match to light a fag
And court extravagance with flowers
That we steal from graves.
Living on the underside, swimming in this borrowed tide
We live on flotsam given up
By the waves.

We the unrespected know our futures are expendable
Our tutors are adversity
Our gods are dead.
Hardly unexpected then that far beyond our mortal ken
A super race of supermen
Are gods instead.

But in our hearts we know the river
Takes back what it gives.
Does the heat of food chain reactions
Provide the light to live?
Does an angel on horseback build a cathedral in the sky?
What are we gonna do when the river runs dry?

We the great unworthy know
That further down this scurvy road
The old familiar pot of gold's already spent.
We put our faith in fairy tales
Of human rights and holy grails
And bang our crucifixion nails until they're bent.

We the underfed and paid are understandably afraid
But hide our fear behind the shade
That hides our light.
But watch now where the shadows fall
Watch them climbing up the wall
They wouldn't be that dark at all without our light.

But in our hearts we know the river
Takes back what it gives.
Does the heat of food chain reactions
Provide the light to live?
Does an angel on horseback build a cathedral in the sky?
What are we gonna do when the river runs dry?

The Colours in the Grey

The sun is shining through the rain
Which falls redundant from the sky
A spectral lullaby
To wash away the pain.
I watch the colours for a while
And the background grey and white
Of clouds is faded out
I listen and I smile.

I hear a drum roll in my mind
A call to action
And I find myself saluting
All the colours in the sky.
A day that starts as good as this
Could never end up like the others
I have suffered
In this wilderness.

I think today is gonna be OK,
I think tomorrow should be good.
I'll keep on thinking of the colours in the grey,
I know that I probably should.

The sun has climbed a little more
I watch the shadows get compressed
As I get dressed
And pick my shades off the floor.
I put them on and leave a note:
'Gone to watch the autumn sky
Gone to watch the leaves get blown around
The ground a bit'.
I stopped, and then I wrote:

I think today is gonna be OK,
I think tomorrow should be good.
I'll keep on thinking of the colours in the grey,
I know that I probably should.

I left the house and felt my pace
Getting quicker
As I walked past the river
With the sun on my face.
The clouds have cried themselves to naught
And the rain is a memory
I smiled as I thought:

I think today is gonna be OK,
I think tomorrow should be good.
I think I'll keep on thinking of the colours in the grey,
I know that I probably should.

Unattainability (the Aphrodisiac of the Sociopath)

You lived your life in a goldfish bowl
I lived mine in a well
You told me you had a second soul
That could break on through my shell
I offered you what I thought you'd asked me for
By then you'd changed your mind
You broke off a bit of me and left me there
Bitter, broken, blind
Bitter, broke and blind

You highlighted parts of me that should be spared
The callous light of day
You could say I was pretty unprepared
For what you had to say
You offered me nothing and I took it all
You took the hope from me
I raised you on a pedestal to watch you fall
You raised a glass to me
Ironically

You taught me how to fly
And then you broke my wings
You were the nonpareil
Of superficial things
You took my destiny
And speared it on a rod
You had me thinking you were God

I wrote you songs of sanctity
You wrote me off as mad
You gave me tea and sympathy
I gave you what I had

I worshipped you where the warships were
Anchored on the Thames
I wanted you as a lover
You loved me as a friend
Or so you would pretend

I thought of you as brandy
You thought of me as brine
You built the walls of your self-esteem
With bricks you stole from mine
You needed me to need you
So you kept me on a string
You wanted me in handcuffs
I wanted you in rings

You taught me how to fly
And then you broke my wings
You were the nonpareil
Of superficial things
You took my destiny
And speared it on a rod
You had me thinking you were God

Urban Tercets for the Street Life

I walked past a bench
In the park, in the hot sun,
And glanced to my right.

King size pack of skins,
Cardboard ripped off for roaches:
I know where you've been.

A small plastic bag
Might once have held some earrings:
Weed is more likely.

Rude boy plus rude girl
Plus a Diamond White bottle
Equals rude baby.

If they got married,
I wonder if their tracksuits
Would match their trainers?

Their language is strange.
Black ghetto kids from the Bronx
Talk in this odd way,

Not Swindon's children.
But they do, English or not.
It asks a question:

Why speak in English?
Why not speak in 'Street'?
Check me, blud, innit?

Hear me, baby girl?
I is talking like I is
One of them black kids.

Isn't this racist?
The old Black and White Minstrels
Impersonate black people,

Their show gets cancelled.
Now a whole generation
Impersonate black people,

And somehow, it's fine.
It doesn't seem fine to me.
It's patronising.

Why is there no show
On reality TV
Taking kids away,

Taking them Bronx-wards
To live that life for real,
To see what it's like?

Kids in real-life gangs
Tend to die in their twenties.
Their life expectancies rise

When they get the chair,
Because there's an eight year wait.
The streets kill in six.

But kids in Swindon
Want the life of a street gang,
They're bored of safety.

Who would want that life?
Surely not those living it.
They'd come like a shot.

They'd come to Swindon
And marvel at everything
We have stopped seeing:

The relatively clean streets,
The virtual lack of street crime,
The unarmed policemen.

Then they'd take over
Because they're harder than us.
Let's not invite them.

We have it easy.
Boring as shit but easy.
Life could be so much worse.

Fond of Rambling Lost in Seven Acres

Despair drips from an hourglass,
The hands click, stopping as each moment passes
To clasp around a cuckoo throat, a noose-child born of pendulum,
A ticking clockwork guillotine as moments like a razor die
To lacerate a memory and frame it on a mantelshelf.

A ticket for a lottery that charred before the draw was made,
Roll up my friend and win a chance
To spend a night in Wonderland,
A timeshare on a lullaby, enraptured seven acres blind,
An all expenses paid bonanza, wrapped in neon,
Wandering a path through tepid possibles
That waltz, meander, beckoning,
And hit a patch of brambles before plunging
through the murky depths
Of circumstance, and casually, indifference like a tidal wave
Resurges and submerges those who looked
too eager, jumped too soon.

Expectation is the nail that's driven through their flailing limbs
To anchor them to resignation, tired of this adventuring.

Icarus and Daedalus have long since split their earthly bonds,
But still the lessons learned of wax have
not been recognised as truth.

The hope that left the feathers tarred
And lit Damascus Boulevard
Grows colder with each second spent
In grasping unattainables.

Comets on elastic leashes grace the sky with pyrotechnic
Pearls of disobedience, a noonday pass to no-man's-land.
Come the evening, welcome home, hi
honey, hope the day was good,
Forget the lunchtime spent atop of someone else's pedestal.

The Norwich Incident

Something interesting happened in Norwich
Fifty years ago.
Somebody looked at the sky
And saw a UFO.

He got off his tractor,
And got on the phone,
To the RAF
And the wife at home,
And said 'help me,
The aliens have come'.

The Sabre jets were scrambled
In the summer sky,
Hunting for an object
Unidentified.

But despite not knowing
If it's good or ill,
They had the orders
'Shoot to kill':
Perhaps it's for the best
It got away.

And when the pilots
Came back down to Earth
No one spoke.
The RAF said
If they mentioned it
Their pilot's licence
Would be revoked.

Is there anybody out there
In the depths of space?

Or is the pinnacle of life in all the universe
The human race?
We're barely walking upright,
Can we really be the best?
I should be proud, I'm just depressed.
I should be proud, I'm just depressed.

Life on Earth is really just coincidence.
So life could still exist somewhere different.
If your nearest star is not too near
You can form the atoms of your atmosphere.
The algae in the oceans will evolve.

Over several aeons complex life appears,
Discovering the wheel and other new ideas.
They get sufficiently advanced
To build a rocket and see the stars:
Perhaps they'll want to come and visit here.

But if I had a rocket of my own
With full control of time and space
And I could choose anywhere to go
I doubt that Norwich would be the place.

Is there anybody out there
In the depths of space?
Or is the pinnacle of life in all the universe
The human race?
We're barely walking upright,
Can we really be the best?
I should be proud, I'm just depressed.
I should be proud, I'm just depressed.

But I want to believe.
Yes, I want to believe.
But I can't believe
'Cause it all seems so naïve.

Three Twelves and a Maybe

Not wanting to be anything, but something that I'm not.
Not knowing what I want, but not wanting what I've got,
I just don't know
Which way to go.
Not wanting to go anywhere, there's nowhere that I can.
Not knowing what I want to be, not wanting what I am,
I just don't know.
I've got to go.

Arrivederci, baby, I've got nothing much to say,
Got three twelves and a maybe anyway.
Three twelves and a maybe and four sevens out of five,
Arrivederci, baby, goodbye.

You tell me that tomorrow's an improvement on today,
I don't know why I still believe you, you said that yesterday,
But nothing's changed.
It's still the same.
You tell me life's a tapestry, a wonder to behold,
You know, it seems more like a travesty, a tragedy,
A hole in which I'll hide
Until I die.

Arrivederci, baby, I've got nothing much to say,
Got three twelves and a maybe anyway.
Three twelves and a maybe and four sevens out of five,
Arrivederci, baby, goodbye.

I used to think that happiness would call on me some day,
Used to think I'd get to know her if she'd settle down and stay,
Guess I was wrong.
Yes, I was wrong.
Depression is a horse I ride, saddled with despair,
Shod with shoes of misery with a mane of scarlet hair

That cuts the wind
And lets her in.
The stableboy was tripping, he forgot to tie the reins,
Now she's galloping unbridled through the meadows of my brain
Out of control.
Please take me home.
I think I might be going somewhere I don't want to go
Think I'd like to leave this journey now
and just return back to home
Please take me home.
Which way is home?

Arrivederci, baby, I've got nothing much to say,
Got three twelves and a maybe anyway.
Three twelves and a maybe and four sevens out of five,
Arrivederci, baby, goodbye.

Oh Death my shadowed saviour, come and free me from this curse
I've had enough of pointless lengthening
my existence on this Earth,
What do you say?
Is that OK?
In the painless vales of nothingness I can hopefully relax
And sympathise with those I left behind to
their misery and their cracked
And broken lives.
Cheer up, you'll die.

So, arrivederci, baby, I've got nothing more to say,
Got three twelves and a maybe anyway.
Three twelves and a maybe and four sevens out of five,
Arrivederci, baby, goodbye, don't cry.
Arrivederci, baby, goodbye.

Hotel Memphis Hard Times Saturday Night

I'm running on empty, my baby has left me,
I thought I'd stepped out of the light.
I dried my last tear as I drank my first beer
And I ordered the next one with ice.
And if you really care, you know I'll be there
At the Hotel Memphis Hard Times Saturday Night.

I brought my guitar, I know I'll go far,
I know the way you taught me the blues.
You wrote me my songs when you treated me wrong
And you know you left me nothing to lose.
So I'll take a shot and I'll gamble the lot
At the Hotel Memphis Hard Times Saturday Night.

I'm going down there, though I've nothing to wear
A Saturday or seven a week.
I'm righting my wrongs as I'm writing my songs
And my heart is kept too sodden to speak.
But it's singing of you and the room with the blues
At the Hotel Memphis Hard Times Saturday Night.

Colours

The tick of a clock in an empty room,
The silence of a prayer.
The toll of a memory bound for a tomb
On the ash of an empty air.
The gasp of an elegy rinsing the wind
Of the eau-de-cologne of time.
The pulse of a neuron, the engine within
The musical box of the mind.

The black of a Sunday, the black of a morn,
The echo of yesterday's choir.
The black of a rosary, gravid as dawn,
The purgative sighing of fire.
The violet of twilight, the grey of a day,
The aquamarine of a wife.
The colour of dreams is a spectrum away
From the rainbow of everyday life.

The puce of a quarrel, the black of a frown,
The sepia-light of regret.
The green of both envy and hippy renown,
The black of a silhouette.
The cyan of silence, the darkness of calm,
The lavender scythe of a choice.
The silence of scream, a contentment alarm
With a woodpecker barb for a voice.

The quickening of anger, the death of a truce,
The dearth of the lights that had shown
The path through the moors where the heart rattled loose
And where black and its sisters were grown.
The tide of a season, the tick of a clock,
The emptiness always pervades.
Just time for the memory e'er tomb is unlocked,
For the colours of living are grey.

Even English Cowboys Get The Blues

I'm sitting on this stony beach,
Staring at the sea,
Feeling all so lonesome and alone.
I'm a cowboy in the Wild East
A Hong Kong Cassidy
And Texas is a million miles from home.
My horse has got asphyxiation
From one too many cars
I thought I'd have to melt him down for glue.
But I took him down the dai pai dong,
Got a hundred bucks and a country song
Called 'Even English Cowboys Get The Blues'.

I got a letter yesterday
My dog has got the flu,
And leprosy and cancer and the mange.
The doctor has investigated
Says he won't pull through
But my woman ran off with him anyway.
My ranch has woodworm, or it did,
Until it all burnt down.
I don't know what the hell I'm gonna do.
So I just pick up my old guitar,
My cowboy hat and my whiskey jar
'Cause I'm just an English cowboy with the blues.

I used to have a rough idea,
Used to have a plan,
Used to dream of riding on the range,
Or sitting in my rocking chair,
Like Willie Nelson's dad
With moonshine taking potshots at my brain.
I used to ride the rodeo

Like I used to ride them gals.
You know I'll always love you Mary Lou.
But my rodeo days upped and went,
When my woman left and my cash got spent,
Now I'm just an English cowboy with the blues.

God I loved that Mary Lou!
She used to have this way
Of dancing that put froth upon my beer.
Her hair was like a beam of gold,
Or ginger anyway,
And I surely miss her bad when she's not here.
But let me tell you something honey,
Let me say it clear:
My cheated heart's been cheating on you too.
You're not the only one you know,
I had Peggy Sue for a buck a go,
And I'm just an English cowboy with the blues.

Barman just another shot
Of red-eye for the road.
I think it's time I'm moseying along.
Think I'll doe-si-doe my lariat
And shuffle off this load.
I'm getting kinda tired of this song.
There's blisters on my fingers now
And cobwebs in my beer.
I might as well be a boy called Sue.
So I'll bid you all a howdy pard
And remember folks, when life gets hard,
At least you're not an English cowboy with the blues.

Insomnia .

The church bell chimes the time
I know it's 3am
I lie awake in the middle of the night
Again

My dreams have haunted me
Sleep is like love
It comes when you're not calling it
Nothing ever changes
Nothing ever stays the same

Night thoughts are predatory
They feed upon your doubts
They do not comfort me
I need to keep them out

Rotating buzzards fill the sky
Above my bed
Their claws extract an eye for an eye
A head for a head

The clock is taunting me
With windmill hands tonight
Its rhythm tortures me
Nothing seems to slow
The grinding of my mind

I try to read
But watch the letters run like rain
No sense in sentences
No meaning on the page

I roll another cigarette
And wish it were a doob
I'm taking moderation to excess

Excessive moderation does nothing
To improve my mood

I check the clock again
Another hour gone
An hour more of purgatory
An hour less 'til dawn

An hour more of gazing
At the fading stars outside
Dawn's rosy middle finger
Lightening the sky

The birds are singing now
Some of them in key
The church bell ringing sounds
Oppressive and funereal
I wonder if it's meant to be?

My mind is racing like
A rabbit from a fox
I close my eyes and see
A bright parade of clocks

I feel like Captain Hook
The ticking makes me weep
I wait on tenterhooks
Say a prayer to Morpheus
And hope that I can get some sleep

Chaos, Love and Infra-Red Excuses

Banged my head against a calendar,
A diary filled with sugar-coated reasons why the days to come
Should differ not from days that passed
Like cattle to an abattoir, deflowered by regret.

The grey of nimbo-cumulus the brightest hue to blacken me
To musings better suited to a cobweb on an hourglass,
A bastard child of Father Time and Mother Nature's sin.

If dreams were seasons, destiny would
lie beneath a wreath of snow,
A Narnian Antarctica awaiting the caress of Spring,
The flaxen smile of daffodil, the maypole's shroud of cotton
And the cuckoo's cool lament for angels cold but not forgotten.

Crystal clear and frozen came the figure
of a mannequin of seraphim,
An icicle ambassador Valhalla-sent
To tempt the lonely masses thronging
printshop bound and wondering
What magic it would take to melt the ice that keeps the Janet in.

If This is it, What Was That?

Will you go where the road takes you
Or will you blow someone else's smoke?
Will you sow your seed on concrete,
Like you never got the joke?
You never drove the Chevy
'Cause the Chevy had a flat.
If this is it, what was that?

You told me you were leaving
I know you've got a new abode.
She can send her begging letters
Where the rubber meets the road.
When you turn the other cheek
There's no turning back.
If this is it, what was that?

It's just a point of view,
It doesn't count for much
But I've never seen the point of you
As such.

I saw you through the window
As you cowered from the rain,
Reflected in the puddles
That collected by the drain.
You were ready for the Chevy
But the Chevy had a flat.
If this is it, what was that?

The Knight was Made for Voodoo

This is a love song inspired by playing the video game 'Gabriel Knight: the Sins of the Fathers'. Unfamiliar words are either locations from the game or Voodoo / Satanic terms. Eg, a vévé is a symbol drawn on the ground to attract spirits. A schattenjaeger is a 'shadow hunter'. A beignet though is just a New Orleans version of a doughnut.

In the alleyway a breeze is blowing
Beignet wrappers from the kerb.
Fat cat sat with a pink martini:
Shaken yes, but not disturbed.
Overhead, the black of nothing
Punctuated by the stars.
Somewhere in this crazy cosmos
Elvis works a noodle bar.

And either the train's a-slowing
Or I'm getting old.
And when I hear the whistle blowing
It cuts me to the bone.
I want to go to Camelot.
Live a chivalric code.
I want to be a schattenjaeger.
Recover my soul.

The skies turn to butter if you look with eyes of straw
And in the dark detritus of a dream
Anything can happen if you tip the boatman more
You can ride it all the way to New Orleans
If you want to.

Drawing baphomets on convent windows,
Silhouetted by the storm.

Crocodile suit and a tribal gris gris
Shadows take on earthly form.
Taking time to sketch the vévé
In the shadow of St Paul's,
You and me together baby,
It's all voodoo after all.

And when I hear those tribal rhythms
My feet misbehave.
And then I start a new beginning
From beyond the grave.
I want to go to Ritterschlosse.
See that teutonic moon
I want to be a schattenjaeger.
If it's not too soon.

The skies turn to butter if you look with eyes of straw,
And in the dark detritus of a dream
Anything can happen if you tip the boatman more
You can ride it all the way to New Orleans.

Meet me in St Louis cemetery number one,
There to drink the brandy of the damned.
Take a train to Pontchartrain to catch the setting sun
And maybe draw our vévé in the sand.

Meet me in the garden where the bougainvillea bloom:
Their blossom falls like flotsam on the shore.
When in the Republic better check the goat for horns:
Je t'aime, mais je n'aime pas cabrit sans cor.

Meet me in the bayou for the rites of St John's Eve
The moonbeams are magenta for a while.
Let me see you dance the python down upon your knees,
But most of all, let me see you smile
'Cause it's over.

Why oh Why oh Why?

Why why write a protest song,
A wailing testament to a world gone wrong?
So the wrong man's dead and the bird has flown.
You can't do shit about it Mr Jones.

Why why bother to care?
It's a crappy old world and you've got your share.
Some bloke you'll never meet has got no home?
You can't do shit about it Mr Jones.

Why should we feed everyone,
All those pot-bellied kids beneath the African sun?
Famine's nature's population control.
You can't do shit about it Mr Jones.

And if you sound optimistic, I guess
It's 'cause you sound simplistic too,
And if you think you've got the answers to it all
I've got a question here for you.

Why why judge hypocrisy?
It's human nature as it ought to be.
You get more stuff if you pawn your soul.
You can't do shit about it Mr Jones.

Why can't the world be like it should?
It's either good at being bad or bad at being good.
Each time the sun comes out, the shadows grow.
You can't do shit about it Mr Jones.

Why why do the bad guys win?
Because they're organised and disciplined.
They learned the rules while you just got stoned.
You can't do shit about it Mr Jones.

And if I sound fatalistic, I guess
It's 'cause I'm pessimistic too.
And if you think you've got the answers to it all
I've got a question here for you.

Why why are so many so poor?
Because society needs them no more.
Their times have changed and their winds have blown.
You can't do shit about it Mr Jones.

Why why am I singing this song?
Don't want to change the world for all that it's wrong.
Your tears of rage could be my next cologne.
You can't do shit about it Mr Jones.

Sic Transit Gloria Monday

Gloria Monday paints her eye
In shadows of regret.
She knows she's easy to remember,
Harder to forget.
The Monday's child is fair of face,
He fresh complexion clear.
She's a model, you know what I mean,
But she's got no idea.

But deep inside, Gloria knows,
Her fifteen minutes wait,
On the other side of rainbows,
The other side of fate.
'Cause she's the face to launch a thousand ships
And she's the legs to sell a thousand slips.
And she's the one to make it
'Cause she's the one to fly.
Sic transit Gloria Monday,
She never wondered why.

Gloria Monday shakes her head,
Spills sequins to the floor.
If this is glamour, give her squalor,
She can't take any more.
Her throat is bloody from bulimia,
Her eyes have lost their glow.
It seemed so easy on the TV,
It seemed so long ago.

But deep inside, Gloria knows,
Her fifteen minutes wait,
On the other side of rainbows,
The other side of fate.

'Cause she's the face to launch a thousand ships
And she's the legs to sell a thousand slips.
And she's the one to make it
'Cause she's the one to fly.
Sic transit Gloria Monday,
She never wondered why.

Mr. and Mrs. Monday put
Their daughter on the train.
They kiss her 'cause they'll miss her
But they won't see her again.
Sixteen hours later
She struts the stage no more.
There's vomit in her windpipe
And she's choking on the floor.

But Gloria knows she's made it
Even though she's gone.
She may have died for vanity
But her name will carry on.
'Cause she's the one who's martyred for her art,
Like Norma Jean, James Dean and Joan of Arc.
And maybe she's remembered
But probably she's not.
Sic transit Gloria Monday
Who ne'er knew where to stop.

Galadriel

Shadows from the passing moon
Of subterranean Middle Earth
Fall eldritch in the afternoon;
The colours slide.
Sitting in an elven glade,
Wrapped in fibres cunning wrought
From juniper, Galadriel
Surveys her pride.

And in the evenings long
Of Lorien's hiatus from the land
She lays her crown aside
To better view the ring upon her hand.
Curiosity calcifies as dream
And so the ring begins to wear the queen.

Ambition's an uneasy friend
Like those in childhood tempting you
To do the things you think you want
But never dare.
Power works like tooth decay
Eroding the enamel
From both temperance and conscience
'Til there's nothing there.

And in a half-remembered elven song
The act begins to play,
Resolution crushed to sand
As the night evicts the day;
A substitution of the black for the green.
And so the ring begins to wear the queen.

One ring to rule them all, one ring to find them,
One ring to bring them all and in the darkness bind them,
In the land of Mordor where the shadows lie.

Galadriel possessed a ring,
Possessed of fell intelligence,
Its power hid Lorien
From prying eyes.
When Frodo from the Shire came,
Bearing one that Sauron made,
Galadriel in elven glade
Surveyed her prize.

Thoughts of treachery and treason spin
Like bats beneath her crown,
The only question which would win the queen
The ultimate renown:
A brace of halflings, or the power supreme?
And so the ring begins to wear the queen.

The Lady laughed, gaining stature,
As the shadows echoed long.
Many moons had she waited
And the chance had come along.
She said to Frodo, as he stifled a scream,
'In throwing down a king you build a queen'.

She raised her hand, and the ring it bore
Issued forth as light.
'I'll be not dark, I'll be beautiful
And dreadful as the night.
As the morning, I'll be terrible and fair.
And everyone shall love me and despair'.

Past enduring was she fair,
Beyond measure was she tall.
But to elven form she fades
When her hand begins to fall.
In a gentle voice, she said she'd passed the test.
And so the queen diminished to the West.

Walking in the Dark

I look over my shoulder
But the past is close behind.
I'm sifting through the ashes
And I'm fairly sure what I will find.
Down beneath the memories lurks
The pain that lets them breathe.
Somewhere in this mortal shell
There beats a heart that wants to leave.

I look out of my window
And appraise the world below.
Out of the corner of periphery,
A taxi driver, moving slow.
Muzak from the lobby
Apprehends my sense of taste.
Back to the comfort of my cubicle,
Booked reluctant left in haste.

And I'm walking in the dark tonight,
The moon has lost her way.
I've had enough of looking on
The bright side of a sunny day.
Give me what I know, at least,
Or give me what I'm due.
I don't know everything I want
But I know that I want you.

Georgia Out of My Mind Suicide Blues

Woke up over Georgia
I must be out of my mind.
I said I woke up over Georgia
Must be out of my mind.
Because I ran out on my woman
Lord knows she ain't the cheating kind.

Lord I hope I die soon
Gotta find some way to ease this pain
I said Lord I hope I die soon
Need to find a way to ease this pain.
'Cause from morning through to night Lord
Can't get that woman out my brain.

Lord show me mercy
Show me the way to forget
Sweet Jesus show me mercy
I need to find me a way to forget
Because Lord I want to die soon
And I ain't even thirty yet.

I've tried all sorts of medicine
I've drank my liquor bottle dry.
I said I've tried all sorts of medicine
I ain't got nothing left to try.
Sweet Jesus show me mercy
And show me sweet Lord how to die.

Fade to Grey

The tick of a clock in an empty room
Monitors temporal flow.
The years go by at the speed of light
But the days take forever to go.
There's a downward swirl in my neural world,
It's been too good for too long.
It's my mandate for being human,
I've got a right to be wrong.

Yesterday I thought today would be the day.
Today I know I'm wrong.
Yesterday, hey hey,
Do you know what you've done?

The speed of time changes all the time,
There must be a black hole around.
And those neutrinos, I think they've seen us
Dipping our heads in the clouds.
The gravity's stronger, the half-life longer,
Howlback down to a trace.
And Schrodinger's cat is clawing back
At the man without a face.

And if you think you know what the hell I'm really saying
Let me know.
'Cause I've got no idea, oh yesterday,
Weren't you supposed to go?

And all the days slip into one after a while
As the colours fade.
And when you think you see the sun going down
I fade to grey.

My spectrum is monochrome robbed of the light.
It's cheaper to watch in black and white.
I live in the shadows I live in the night.
I fade to grey.

And all the days slip into one after a while
As the colours fade.
And when you think you see the sun going down
I fade to grey.
I fade to grey.

The Road

The road ahead has got no signs,
No clues to where to go.
And there's no dotted lines
So people drive both sides,
And when it's dark, too dark to see,
You still can smell your way.
The ash of gasoline
Will keep you walking straight.

Thought of buying me a map,
A travel magazine,
But where I really want to go
No one's ever been.
You find your own way if you can,
Some people never will,
The fear of leaving somewhere safe
Will keep them blinkered still.

And on we go down this wasted road
On this trip into the unknown.
And soon enough we get broken up
And I end up walking on my own.
Sometimes I feel like going home.
Sometimes,
But not often.

The river flows beneath the bridge
And on towards the sea
And as it passes out of reach
It passes over me.
And when you're living on the edge
You've found your rightful place
'Cause he not living on the edge
Is taking too much space.

And on we go down this wasted road
On this trip into the unknown.
And soon enough we get broken up
And I end up walking on my own.
Sometimes I feel like going home.
Sometimes,
But not often.

Sestina Siesta

*A sestina is a poem where the same set of six words ends the
lines of each stanza but in a different (and predetermined)
order each time. These words are then included in a three-
line stanza at the end, again in a predetermined order.*

The old man turned his hat brim to the Sun
And wondered when his mind had turned from Summer.
His rocking chair squeaked as he reached for his beer, lazy
And lethargic, the sun's unforgiving glare making him hot.
He felt a prickling: was he starting to burn?
He wished he could get to the van in time for some ice cream.

But by the time he got there, the ice cream
Van would have gone, leaving him standing foolishly in the Sun,
Another unwanted item by the side of the road, waiting to burn.
He cast his mind back, the Ghost of Summer
Past adding flesh to his memories: back then, it was hot
But he never felt this lazy.

He watched the kids in his neighbour's garden. They weren't lazy:
Fuelled by Coke, fuelled by ice cream,
They ran like banshees, screaming and throwing water. They weren't hot
Because they were irrigated. They splashed in the pool and
                                        laughed at the Sun:
They had not learnt reasons to fear Summer
And the anxiously-applied factor fifty would prevent sun burn.

The old man's granddaughter worked through her sun burn.
Her back was peeling and prickling: her friends were lazy
And she had no boyfriend to ask when her back needed the
                                        coat of Summer,
The basting of herself in sun cream.
She is a redhead and knows to fear the Sun
But it's sometimes hard to tell it can be so hot.

She sits in her call centre cubicle, fan in her face, it is so hot,
Trying to sit where the hessian chair won't hurt her sun burn.
She has a love-hate relationship with the Sun:
She loves it and it hates her. Now she feels lazy,
Indolent and immolated, the after-sun cream
Marking the turf of her war with another Summer.

The weather girl smiles ever broader because this is Summer
And we are supposed to like weather that is hot.
Smile on, weather girl, like the cat that got the cream:
You don't look like you burn.
You don't look like you have been lazy
In your flesh-sacrifice to the god of the Sun.

The cream of British weather is its Autumn, not its Summer.
Yes, there are some who like the Sun hot
But there are probably more who burn, more still who just feel lazy.

Summer is indeed a bummer.

Scissors in My Satchel

I'm walking out backwards my porch last night
Sitting with a drink for an alibi
Blues in my pocket and my head in the sand
Coughing up blood like a dying man
Scissors in my satchel gonna
Cut me some slack tonight

Busy running sideways from a flashing light
Cigarettes and rizla with a breeze to fly
Razor blades and sunlight on the stereo
Payable reminders on the telephone
Scissors in my satchel gonna
Cut me some slack tonight

Silverfish and goldfish give a diamond back
Spayed clubs, dime-a-dozen heart attacks
Blues in the belfry and my moon in Mars
Lying 'bout the gutter when you're shooting stars
Scissors in my satchel gonna
Cut me some slack tonight

Caveats from Habitat adorn the walls
Ottoman called Helga and a bed called Bjorn
Daydream believer you believe in sand
Trying to keep the tide out with your grasping hands
Scissors in my satchel gonna
Cut me some slack tonight

Singing for your supper 'til the waiter dies
Trading in the gravel for a taste of sky
Blues at my table with a sabre drawn
A Rockwell breakfast for a cartoon dawn
Scissors in my satchel gonna
Cut me some slack tonight

Drum machines and denim under neon skies
Styrofoam Delilahs living plastic lies
Razor rash and hairgel in a paisley tie
Everyone's a winner 'cause it's free all night
Scissors in my satchel gonna
Cut me some slack tonight

Time's Diode

We move
In a straight line
Through the fractal wonderland
Of universal time.

Today's the tomorrow of yesterday,
Time just goes so fast.
One future of two days ago
Is one day in the past.

The future is ineffable,
The past can't be recalled.
The present is just fictional:
It don't exist at all.

I'm a time traveller, baby,
It took twenty-four hours,
But I travelled here from this time yesterday.
I'm a time traveller, baby,
This time yesterday's no more.
This time tomorrow's on its way.

The future is consumed and is
Excreted as the past.
Every living creature has its own.
Nothing is less absolute,
More arbitrary than time,
Individual perceptions
Categorise what they've been shown.

I'm going on a mission
Wish me luck before I go.
I'm travelling to a future
That I still don't want to know.

I'd offer you a lift
On my trip through time and fate
But we're on the same trajectory
Moving at the same damned rate,

We're all time travellers, baby,
Trudging future-bound through time.
The fourth dimension has the least control.
I'm a time traveller, baby,
The pendulum's my heart,
And the Amazonian butterfly that flutters is my soul.

I'm a time traveller, baby,
It took twenty-four hours,
But I travelled here from this time yesterday.
I'm a time traveller, baby,
This time yesterday's no more.
This time tomorrow's on its way.

The Money God

The kingdom, the power, the glory is mine,
Forever, whenever, the passing of time.
The woven-knit clothing, the shirt on your back:
It's mine for the taking, I'm taking it back.

The song in your heart and the spring in your step
And your satellite dish and your video set
And the food in your fridge and the drugs in your veins:
Kneel down to your master, you'll get them again.

For I am the Money God, by my will you live.
Food, shelter, clothing, mine only to give.
For mine is the kingdom and mine is the crown:
You're mine for the taking, I'm taking you now.

I want a sacrifice.
I want you heart and soul and brain.
Can't you feel me
In blood and bone and vein?
Kneel before me
Your petty life at my command.
Adore me.
Loving me's not hard.

I'm your faith, your hope, your sanity,
Your collar and your chain.
The spade that lays your ghosts to rest
Then digs them up again.
The hand that steals from children's mouths
The food you bled to buy.
The law that tells you how to live
But gives no reason why.

For I am the Money God and my word is law.
I'm what you're living, dying, crying, lying, fighting for.
I'm the one that breaks the spirit, burns
the bridges, digs the grave,
Turns the key that ties the blindfold and
grants madness to the sane.

For I am the Money God, your Master, your Lord,
The hawk that's a handsaw, the flower that's a sword.
The Pandora's box that unlocks your despair.
The foot 'neath the noose after kicking the chair.

The cancer, the virus that tears you apart,
The blight on your conscience, the stain on your heart,
The abandoned subversion, the relics of will,
The blood and the bones on the butterfly wheel.

For I am the Money God, immortal, divine.
No nation's foundation is greater than mine.
No heart has the power not to rise to my call
For greed is my army, and greed conquers all.

O worthless and weak with your empires of sand,
On the granite of want does my empire stand,
On the song of the soldier, the banker, the whore:
'I'll give you my life if you give me some more'.

For I am the road that you'll walk 'til you die,
'Til the worms are your bedfellows, the sodden earth your sky,
'Til your soul is set free and you cast off your chains
And a blanket of daisies is all that remains.

But I am the Money God, untouched by it all.
My empire grows with each child that is born.
My kingdom is boundless, my reign without end.
Forever. And ever. And ever. Amen.

I Am the Rain

I'm sitting in this crowded house looking at the rain,
Watching crested rivulets form patterns on the pane.
I'm thinking of another place, I'm thinking of a time.
Life had seemed so simple when I thought I'd made it mine.

I set my mind in motion making forays for the door.
There had to be an answer if I knew what I was looking for.
There's something in the air tonight, a carrot on a chain.
Set the plan in motion and release the dogs again.

I am the rain.
I feel myself come falling.
I fell again.
And now the only sun
Is the one that I am running from.

The roof could do with fixing and the gutter's coming down.
The rain that made the flowers grow has
brought the temple crashing down.
There's acid in its essence, but a rainbow in the sky.
Take the time to gamble or the world goes washing by.

The clouds have choked the sunlight from this vision of the sky.
Shadows reach cold fingers for the truth behind the alibi.
Somewhere in the darkness, there's a candle being lit,
And somewhere in the cloudburst, there's
the sound of someone's kiss.

I am the rain.
I feel myself come falling.
I fell again.
And now the only sun
Is the one that I am running from.

Where is the Hope?

Where is the hope?
Because now I know
Where the despair is,
I have forgotten
That there is a bright side to life.
I now understand
More than I want to.
And if the dark side takes over
I cannot stop it
And if the sun comes out
It is not for long.
Storm clouds fill the sky but
Aren't they supposed to go soon?
Despair and gloom came to visit but
Seem to have moved in.
A new perspective, a new outlook
Will never happen
Despair taking over:
It is inevitable.

But almost nothing is really inevitable, and everything is just a
matter of perspective, as reading this upwards will show...

Poetry Rivals - About Us

Poetry Rivals was founded in 2009 with the aim of taking poetry from the page on to the stage. We received in excess of 7,000 entries for our first Poetry Rivals competition on a huge array of subjects and produced a collection of fantastic books from all ages and walks of life.

Andrew Barber beat 49 other finalists to take the first ever Poetry Rivals Winner's crown and Cleo Henry (14) was our under 18s winner. This collection proves that taking risks and rising to challenges can fulfil ambitions.

For more information on Poetry Rivals please visit our website www.poetryrivals.com. You can email us at info@poetryrivals.com or give us a call on 01733 890099.

Poetry Rivals
Remus House
Coltsfoot Drive
Woodston
Peterborough
PE2 9JX